ISBN 978-0-282-99041-1
PIBN 10875946

1 MONTH OF
FREE
READING

at

www.ForgottenBooks.com

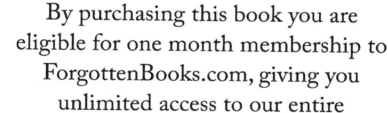

By purchasing this book you are
eligible for one month membership to
ForgottenBooks.com, giving you
unlimited access to our entire
collection of over 1,000,000 titles via
our web site and mobile apps.

To claim your free month visit:
www.forgottenbooks.com/free875946

English
Français
Deutsche
Italiano
Español
Português

www.forgottenbooks.com

Mythology Photography **Fiction**
Fishing Christianity **Art** Cooking
Essays Buddhism Freemasonry
Medicine **Biology** Music **Ancient**
Egypt Evolution Carpentry Physics
Dance Geology **Mathematics** Fitness
Shakespeare **Folklore** Yoga Marketing
Confidence Immortality Biographies
Poetry **Psychology** Witchcraft
Electronics Chemistry History **Law**
Accounting **Philosophy** Anthropology
Alchemy Drama Quantum Mechanics
Atheism Sexual Health **Ancient History**
Entrepreneurship Languages Sport
Paleontology Needlework Islam
Metaphysics Investment Archaeology
Parenting Statistics Criminology
Motivational

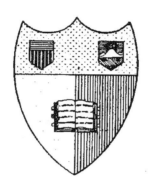

A MANUAL OF THE ELECTRO-CHEMICAL TREATMENT OF SEEDS

A MANUAL OF THE ELECTRO-CHEMICAL TREATMENT OF SEEDS

BY

CHARLES MERCIER, M.D.

F.R C.P., ETC.

"He gave it for his opinion that whoever could make two ears of corn, or two blades of grass, to grow upon a spot of ground where only one grew before, would deserve better of mankind, and do more essential service to his country, than the whole race of politicians put together."

A Voyage to Brobdingnag.

LONDON

UNIVERSITY OF LONDON PRESS, LTD.

18 WARWICK SQUARE, E.C.4

1919

PREFACE

WHEN I first heard, about a year ago, of the electrification of seeds, and was told that it produced an increase in the crop grown from seed so treated, I naturally put the statement down as moonshine. My information came, however, from persons of standing and experience in the world of agriculture, who had, as far as I knew, no axe to grind, and were evidently convinced of the truth of their belief; and it seemed worth while, therefore, to investigate the evidence in order to undeceive them, for the thing was on the face of it incredible.

Fortunately, no knowledge of agriculture was needed. All that was necessary was ability to investigate evidence in a proper critical spirit—and the critical spirit was certainly not wanting. But soon a wonder came to light. The further I carried my investigations, the more difficult I found it to maintain my sceptical attitude. At length, being in danger of a conversion parallel with that of Balaam the son of Beor, and mistrusting my own judgment, I induced several parties of experienced agriculturists, occupying responsible positions, to visit the fields at harvest-time and form their own opinions. These gentlemen, experts appointed by foreign governments, agricultural correspondents of influential newspapers, landowners cultivating thousands of acres of their own land, and so forth, accordingly visited the farms, and examined the crops growing from treated and untreated seed side by side. In not one case was the opinion adverse to the process. In nearly every case it was very favourable, and in some it was enthusiastic.

After this, I was obliged to revise my attitude ; and having regard to the serious shortage of food that threatened, and still threatens, not this country only, but the whole world, I determined to spread the knowledge of the process as widely as I possibly could.

It was true that the process was patented, and that I was not financially interested in it ; but I did not see that the financial benefit that my efforts might bring to the inventor was any reason why the country should not reap full benefit from the invention. If the labourer is worthy of his hire, surely the inventor is worthy of his reward. Seven years of strenuous work and the expenditure of thousands of pounds may surely look for some reward without being considered sordid.

CHAS. MERCIER.

CONTENTS

A MANUAL OF THE ELECTRO-CHEMICAL TREATMENT OF SEEDS

CHAPTER I

HISTORY

THE application of electro-chemistry to agriculture and horticulture is quite new. The application of electricity to plants for the purpose of stimulating their growth is indeed of long standing. Forty years ago Sir William Siemens applied electricity to growing crops, and was followed by the Berthelots, father and son, who conducted long series of experiments. Later still, other physicists took up the matter, and of late years it has even attracted the attention of the Board of Agriculture, in whose journal records of experiments have

appeared from time to time since 1910.   It
is important to keep in mind the difference
between the application of electricity alone
to growing crops and the application of an
electro-chemical process to seed before it is
sown.   The distinction is clear enough, but
the two processes are constantly confused,
and the electro-chemical process is supposed
to be the same as the electric process, or a
mere unimportant variation of it.

In. the electric process, no application of
electricity is made to the seed before germination takes place.   In the electro-chemical
process, the sole application of electricity
is made to the ungerminated seed.   In the
electric process, chemicals are not used :
electricity alone is applied to the crop.   In
the electro-chemical process, the seed is
steeped in a solution of some metallic salt,
and the passage of the electricity through
the solution drives the ions of the salt into
the seed.   The process is not solely electrical, but is electro-chemical, inasmuch as it
utilises electricity to produce a chemical

Mr Hill's Works at Poole.   Interior, showing treated seed on the drying floor.   The basket han ˙   from the

result, though it must be understood that this is not the whole result. In the electric process, the electricity is not applied until the plant has appeared above ground, and is then applied more or less continuously throughout the whole period of growth of the plant. It is discontinued at night, and in rainy weather, but is applied daily, as far as weather will permit, from the time of appearance of the plant above ground until harvest. In the electro-chemical process, the electricity is applied to the seed once for all, before it is even sown. It is passed through the seed alone for a few hours, and then the operation is at an end. In the electric process, posts are set up on the ground on which the crop is grown, wires are carried from post to post, and electricity must be brought into the farmer's fields. In the electro-chemical process, the farmer's fields are not invaded. The apparatus may be miles away; the farmer has nothing to do with the matter except to send his seed to the electrifying station;

and after he has received it back again, all his farming operations proceed in the usual manner. A project is now on foot for sending a travelling apparatus round to the farms, so that even the necessity of sending away the seed to be treated will be abolished. From what has been said it will be seen that the two processes are entirely different, having nothing whatever in common but the use of electricity—and even this is used at a very different amperage and voltage.

The application of electricity to growing crops has been tried experimentally by various experimenters for at least forty years. The application of an electro-chemical process to seeds is quite new. Until Mr Fry began his experiments about seven years ago, it does not appear that any attempt had been made to apply such a process to seeds, or to use any electrolytic process in agriculture or horticulture.

The inventor of the Wolfryn electro-chemical process had been for many years interested in electricity, and had directed his

Paris and London Photo Agency.

Mr Hill's Works at Poole for electrification of seeds—Exterior.

attention to the production of high-tension electricity by means of steam, turning to practical use a discovery of Faraday's that had lain neglected ever since his experiments revealed the possibility. Mr Fry designed an apparatus by which he was able to produce at very small cost oscillating currents of enormous tension, up to as high as 100,000 volts. The apparatus was so successful and so cheap that it afforded means of equipping every tramp steamer with a wireless apparatus, and in fact was used successfully on an experimental scale by one of the steamers of the Great Western Railway Company plying between Weymouth and the Channel Isles. The Admiralty sent down members of its wireless department to investigate the matter, and successful trials were made. When this point was reached, however, and a great future appeared to be opened out for the application of the invention, it was found impossible to use it without employing transmitters and receivers that were already protected by Marconi's patents, and it was necessary to abandon the project, at any rate until these patents had lapsed.

It was then suggested to Mr Fry that he should turn his attention to the application of electricity produced by steam to growing crops. He knew of what had been done in this direction, and on mature consideration he arrived at the conclusion that, however experimentally successful the application of high-tension currents to growing crops might be, the expense of the application was such that it could not be made economically beneficial, and he made no attempt to pursue this matter. But his mind having been directed to the application of electricity to agriculture, it occurred to him to try its effect upon seed. If, as appeared to be established, electricity exerted a beneficial effect upon the growth of plants in their maturer stages, it was possible, and even probable, that it might stimulate the germination of seeds also. This was a fairly obvious inference; but it was a much longer step, and one that few would have thought of making, to conjecture that the electrification of seed before it is sown might produce such a change in the seed as to cause it to germinate earlier when subsequently sown, and to produce a more healthy, vigorous, and fertile plant. This was a totally new conception. There were no known facts either in support of it or in conflict with it, and the only thing to be done was to follow the maxim of John Hunter.—Don't think : try.

Here, however, occurred the first difficulty. If currents of high tension, such as the inventor had been experimenting with, were passed into the grain, the apparatus required would be very expensive and complicated and would need an expert to work it. It would be desirable, therefore, to use ordinary low-tension electricity. But ordinary low-tension electricity would not have the penetrating power of high-tension electricity, and would not be able to penetrate the seed without the aid of a conducting medium. Such a medium would be furnished by a

Paris and London Photo Agency.

Oats grown by Mr Legg, Blashenwell Farm, Corfe Castle. Electrified on the
left unelectrified on the right. The number of straws in each bundle is

solution of some metallic salt, and hence the advisability of steeping the seed in such a solution, and of passing the electricity through the seed while it is immersed. The current would of course have an electrolytic effect on the solution, would decompose it and drive its ions into the seed immersed in it. Hence the process would no longer be a purely electrical process : it would become in part a chemical process ; it would be electro-chemical. And thus the electro-chemical treatment of seeds originated.

If a solution of a salt must be used, it was natural to choose first those that are used for the purpose of chemical manures, the most soluble of which are sulphate of ammonia and nitrate of soda, and these are also fairly abundant and fairly cheap. Nitrate of soda was first used. Wheat was steeped in a solution of the salt, electricity of low tension was passed through it for a good many hours, and then the wheat was sown in large pots, at the same time with untreated wheat in other pots, filled with similar soil, for control, and the two were placed side by side in the open air for comparison. The result was awaited with a good deal of curiosity ; and when it was found that in all the pots of treated wheat the seeds germinated earlier than in the control pots, it appeared that the treatment had produced some effect ; and this impression was confirmed later on, when the plants from the treated seed grew stronger, taller, and produced better ears and more of them. Here was a beginning that encouraged further investigation. It seemed to show that the process was worth following up. It held out hopes of good results to be obtained in time.

In the following season more numerous trials were made. Oats and barley were added to the seeds experimented on. Larger quantities were treated. Solutions of several different salts were employed, and in each solution different lots of seeds were treated for different lengths of time. The quantities treated were now too large to be sown in pots, and a piece of arable land was set aside and marked out into plots, on each of which a sample of the electro-chemically treated corn was sown, a neighbouring plot being in every case sown with untreated seed of the same sample at the same time, for comparison and control. Again when harvest time came round the results were decidedly encouraging : the electrified seed gave better crops than the controls. But the results were not uniform. Some of the plots showed better results than others, and reference to the records afforded an indication as to what length of treatment, what strength of current, what kind of solution, and so forth, afforded the best result.

It is evident that the permutations and combinations of these several factors are very numerous ; and as the three kinds of seed, wheat, oats, and barley, were experimented on, the number of experiments was trebled. In each solution, and in each separate strength of solution, different samples of each seed were treated for half an hour, for an hour, for an hour and a half, for two hours, and so on, and with different strengths of current. The several samples were then sown, always with a control plot sown at the same time, and the results awaited. The method was very tedious, since only one crop could be raised in each season, and there was no previous experience, there were no former experiments of the same kind, to take for guidance : the inventor was obliged to begin at the very beginning.

Little by little the conditions were narrowed down. Little by little the proper treatment began to emerge ; and the first conclusions were rather surprising. It was found that, although the seeds of wheat, oats, and barley are so much alike in size, shape, consistency, and in all belonging to the same natural order of Gramineæ, yet they did not respond to the treatment in the same way. In order to secure the best result in barley, it had to be treated for twice as long as oats, which it so closely resembles. It was found that the constitution of the electrodes made a material dif-

Paris and London Photo Agency

Oats grown by Mr R. S. Hunt, in the same field at Poundbury
The electrified, on the left, were sown

ference, iron electrodes producing a better effect than carbon. It was found that common salt made a very good medium, though not the best, to steep the grain in ; and it was found that seed treated in solution of one salt was better adapted to one kind of soil, and produced a better crop when sown therein than the same seed when treated in a solution of a different salt ; while with other soils the success was reversed. Evidently the affair was becoming extremely complicated. Hundreds of experiments were made every season, and the total number is now very large ; but still, even for the three staple cereals there is yet much to be discovered, and the investigation of the proper treatment of horticultural seeds is scarcely more than begun. Enough has been done with them to show that when full investigations have been made, and the proper treatment for each seed determined, results as good as those already obtained with cereals may be confidently expected. But up to the present the main efforts of the inventor have been concentrated upon determining with accuracy the best treatment for cereals; and when it is borne in mind how many factors are to be determined, and that the right combination of all these factors must be separately determined for each kind of seed in each kind of soil, the wonder is, not that so little has been determined for horticultural seeds, but that so much has been determined with respect to cereals.

Even for cereals much remains to be done. There are something like 150 different kinds of wheat in cultivation, and it is quite probable that, although every kind of wheat yields superior crops when treated in the manner ascertained as appropriate for wheat in general, yet each kind would yield better results still if it received a special treatment peculiarly suited to its own peculiar constitution. It will be seen, therefore, that the investigation is practically endless, and that many years must elapse before the treatment that is perfectly appropriate to all the common garden seeds is known. On the other hand, it must be remembered that all that has been achieved at present has been achieved by the efforts of but a single investigator, working at first in the dark, and doing everything, from the preparation of the soil to the sowing and harvesting of the seed, for himself. From his numerous experiments principles are beginning to emerge into view. It is beginning to be possible to say, "Seed of this kind will take about so long to treat ; such and such a combination of salts will be found, if not the best, yet somewhere near the best"; and so forth. As these principles become more clearly and firmly established, the time occupied in investigating the treatment of any particular kind of seed will be shortened ; and when many investigators are employed in a college with a proper staff of subordinates to undertake the routine duties, investigation will proceed faster still. But it is not possible at present to look forward to a time when such a staff will come to the end of its labours.

The kinds of seeds used in agriculture alone are numerous, and those used in horticulture are perhaps twenty, perhaps fifty times as numerous ; and of all these, only three, the staple cereals grown in this country, have been sufficiently tested to warrant the commercial use of the process upon them.   There are other cereals, such as rye, millet, sesame, rice, etc., whose treatment is not yet determined, and the determination of the treatment of even the commonest of horticultural seeds is scarcely yet begun.

It is scarcely begun, and for none of these seeds has the correct mode of treatment been fully ascertained.   But something has been done ; some trials have been made, and for some of these seeds the trials have been fairly extensive, and up to the present no seed has been found that has not benefited by electrification. Applications have been made from distant parts of the world for trials to be made upon rice, sugar-cane, cotton, flax, and other seed ; and though, as has been said, the application of the process to these seeds has not been worked out in detail, yet up to the present no kind of seed has been found that does not respond to the treatment by producing a more vigorous plant, richer and superior in quality in some respect for which it is cultivated. This is especially true of cotton, tobacco, root crops such as mangels, turnips, and swedes, cabbages, tomatoes, and some others. All these crops are grown as annuals, and are harvested within a twelvemonth after they are sown ; and it is probable that for such crops the process will be found more beneficial than for crops that do not come to maturity until after a longer interval from sowing time, such as orchids, pepin fruits (apples and pears), citron fruits (oranges, lemons, and citrons), bush fruits (raspberries, gooseberries, currants), brambles (blackberries, logan-berries, wine-berries), and other cultivated crops. We do not yet know whether these crops of a longer maturation period will be benefited by the process, but all of them are occasionally grown from seed for the production of new varieties, and at present the process is a very tedious one, for years elapse before the plant grown from hybridised seed reaches the fruiting stage, so that the qualities of its fruit can be estimated. If, as may fairly be anticipated, this period of waiting can be shortened by a season or two, it is evident that the commercial advantage will be considerable.

It has been said above that crops grown from seed that has been treated by the electro-chemical process are superior both in quantity and quality to those grown from untreated seed of the same sample. The quality of corn is estimated by its weight, and a small difference in the weight of a bushel indicates a considerable difference in the quality of the corn. A poor sample of wheat weighs 60 lbs. per bushel, an average sample 62 or 63 lbs. per bushel, a fine sample 64 lbs. per bushel, and 65 lbs. per bushel is an extraordinarily fine sample, such as is

Paris and London Photo Agency.

Oats grown by Mr Roseveare, Gains Cross Farm, Blandford.   Electrified

seen only in exceptional seasons. Now, the increase in weight observed in wheat grown from electrified seed varies from 1 to 4 lbs. per bushel. It is evident, therefore, that the use of the process not only increases the bulk of the crop, but also so improves its quality that it may command a higher price per bushel, yield more flour and less offal, and that wheat that would otherwise be fit for milling purposes alone may become fit for seed.

This is a sample of the improvement in quality, but it is only a sample. Cotton grown from electrified seed produces a longer staple, and length of staple is one of the most important qualities of cotton. On the other hand, tobacco grown from electrified seed produces immense leaves that are not always of as good a quality as the smaller leaves grown from unelectrified seed.

It is not only true seeds that yield better crops when electrified. Potatoes also yield a more abundant crop when the " seed " potatoes have been subjected to the process before they are set in the ground, and experiments are now being made with bulbs. Though the increase in the crop of potatoes has been very pronounced, it has not been constant. Sometimes the crop produced from electrified potatoes has shown a diminution, showing that in these cases the process had not been properly performed and that the true conditions required by potatoes had not been observed. The same untoward result was occasionally produced in the early experiments on cereals, before the best conditions had been ascertained ; and there is no reason to doubt that as soon as the best conditions for electrifying potatoes have been ascertained, success in increasing the crop will be as uniformly secured with potatoes as it already is with cereals. For the moment, however—that is, until another season has passed and provided its experience,—the expectation with respect to increase in the crop of potatoes can be looked on only as extremely promis-

Paris and London Photo Agency.

Black Tartarian oats, grown by Mr W. F. Smith on Mrs Duke's Farm, Godmanstone. Electrified on the left, unelectrified on the right. 75 straws in each bundle. The difference. both in straw and grain. is conspicuous.

ing, not as assured. The inventor will, however, welcome the trial of experimental plots of electrified potatoes, provided always that unelectrified seed potatoes of the same sample are planted at the same time, in the same field, and under the same conditions, so that a fair comparison can be made.

CHAPTER II

THE PROCESS

THE nature of the process has already been sketched. It is the passage of a weak current of electricity for a certain length of time through the seed, the duration of the treatment varying with the kind of seed treated. As a weak current of electricity will not pass through dry seed, the seed must be steeped in water; and as a weak current will not pass readily through tap water, some salt must be dissolved in the water to render it conductive. Any salt will render the water a conductor, but not every salt produces the same effect upon the seed. The salts most readily procured are common salt and chloride of calcium, and with these the majority of the experi-

Paris and London Photo A

ments have been made and the whole of the farmers' seed has been treated. Other salts have been tried, and remarkable effects have followed; but most of the experiments have been conducted during the war, and the war has made some salts too expensive for use upon a large scale, and has made others altogether unprocurable. Hence common salt (chloride of sodium) and chloride of calcium have been the salts used. The solutions have been used at a strength of from 2½ to 5 per cent., the solid being taken by weight and the liquid by measure, so that 1 oz. of salt is used for each pint of water, ½ lb. for each gallon. The quantity of the solution required is 5 gallons or more per bushel of seed, so that a charge of 50 sacks of seed would require 1000 gallons of solution.

In practice, the solution and the seed are best contained in an oblong shallow tank, which may be of wood, or concrete, or brick faced with cement. In any case, the internal angles should be rounded, to facilitate the removal of every grain of seed when

Paris and London Photo Agency.

Oats from the same field Electrified on the left, unelectrified
on the right. The same number of straws in each bundle.
The difference is conspicuous.

the operation is over, and the floor should slope from all directions to a drain, the aperture of which must be closed by a wire grid, to prevent the escape of the seed when the liquor is drawn off by opening a valve in the course of the drain.

A tank of the inside measurement of 6 ft. 6 in. × 3 ft. × 2 ft. deep will treat 4 sacks at one charge. A tank 8 ft. × 4 ft. × 2 ft. 6 in. deep will take a charge of 10 sacks. A tank 10 ft. × 5 ft. × 3 ft. will take a charge of 20 sacks; and so on. As a matter of practical convenience it is found better to have several small tanks than one large one.

Each end of the tank is completely faced on the inside with an iron plate $\frac{1}{8}$ inch thick, which serves as an electrode, and to these plates the wires conveying the electricity are attached.

The source of the electricity may be a dynamo installed for the purpose, or it may be a town supply. In either case a switchboard is necessary, with a rheostat for regulating the current. The quantity of electricity employed for most seeds is about 8 watts per gallon of fluid used. A good working rule is to allow 2 amperes per square foot of acting surface of one electrode. The tanks may be ranged in series or in parallel, as may be most convenient.

After the seed has received its proper quantum of current, which varies much according to the kind under treatment, the liquor is run off and the seed is taken out and conveyed to the drying apparatus.

Wet seed cannot be sown. It sticks together, and if an attempt is made to sow it broadcast it falls in lumps instead of in separate grains, and for the same reason it will not pass through the drills. Even if not wet, but only damp—though the seed may be sown if not very damp,—it is swollen, will not pass through the drills at all unless they are suitably adjusted, and even then will not pass regularly and equally. Moreover, a farmer must sow his seed, not when he would, but when he can—that is to say, when he has produced a good seed-bed, and

Paris and London Photo Agency

Primitive tanks for ten sacks each. used in the early stages of the process.

when the weather is favourable. It is rare, therefore, for a farmer to be able to sow his seed the day that he receives it, and if it is kept in a damp state it may heat, so that its germinating power is destroyed ; or it may sprout, and become unsowable ; or, if neither of these accidents happens, it is sure to become mildewed, and thereby injured. For all these reasons it is necessary to dry the seed.

But there is another cogent reason. It is well known to practical farmers that the drying of damp seed equalises and stimulates its germination, and the crop is slightly improved if the seed is merely soaked and then dried. The crop is still further improved if the seed is dried after being soaked in certain chemical solutions ; and the improvement has been occasionally such that the inventor of the electro-chemical process has taken out a patent for the process of soaking in chemicals and drying. But this was done chiefly as a safeguard, for the resulting improvement is never so great as is obtained by the additional process

Paris and London Photo Agency.

Barley grown by Mr Roseveare, Gains Cross Farm, Blandford.   Elec-

of electrification, and when once the seed is in the salted liquor, and the necessary expense of subsequent drying has been incurred, it adds little to the trouble or the expense to pass a current of electricity through the seed, and thus gain the maximum of benefit.

The seed must be dried, and the drying is very important. If the seed is not sufficiently dried, it not only loses the benefit that is derived, as has just been mentioned, from being dried, but it may become mildewed or mouldy or otherwise damaged. On the other hand, if it is dried too much it may be killed outright. Every organised structure, every part of an animal or vegetable body, contains a certain share of moisture, and if deprived of this moisture it dies. Seed corn contains naturally from 11 to 14 per cent. of moisture, and if it is deprived of this residual moisture it dies. It is important, therefore, that the seed should not be over-dried.

The method usually employed for the

drying of various substances is the application of heat, and it is usually supposed that the application of heat is sufficient by itself to extract or drive the moisture out of the heated substance ; and many commercial appliances for drying are constructed on the principle that heating is sufficient for drying. This is a mistake, and is in some appliances a very costly mistake. Heat is a useful assistant and adjuvant to drying, but heat by itself is totally useless.

If we fill a vessel with water and then close the vessel air-tight, so that nothing can escape, it is manifest that we may heat it to any degree we please and the water will not escape so long as the vessel is strong enough to withstand the pressure. Or if, instead of water, we fill the vessel with wet clothes or wet corn or any other wet substance, the same is true. If we heat the vessel, the wet clothes or the wet corn will be heated, but will not be dried. They will not be dried, for the moisture cannot escape, and when the vessel is opened, the only difference will be that the clothes or the corn, instead of being cold and wet, will be hot and wet. They will still be as wet as ever.

On the other hand, everyone knows the drying effect of a March wind. A peck of March dust is worth a king's ransom, and fortunately there is usually much dust in March, and dust is dry—very dry. How is it that this soil which was moist, unpleasant mud yesterday is dry dust to-day? It has not been heated. March wind is not hot: it is very cold—nothing makes one shiver as March wind does. But yet it is a most powerful drier. Why? Manifestly because, though it is not hot, it is dry.

If a thing is wet—that is to say, if it has moisture adhering to its surface—this moisture may be removed by wiping, or by blotting, or by centrifugalising, or by evaporation; but if the substance is damp—if, that is to say, the moisture is not in the surface but inherent in the texture of the substance—then this moisture can be removed by evaporation into the air and in no other way. The moisture in the substance is under tension—that is to say, its particles are in movement, and in the course of this movement they are constantly coming to the surface and tending to fly off. Whether or not they will fly off depends entirely upon whether there is room for them in the adjacent air. Air can hold a great deal of water vapour, but cannot hold an indefinitely large quantity ; and when it is full, it can hold no more. If we put a moist substance into air that is saturated with moisture, the substance will not dry ; but if the air is not saturated, it will take up moisture until it becomes saturated ; and the drier it is, the more rapidly it will take up moisture, and the more rapidly a moist substance placed in it will become dry. But, of course, as the moisture escapes from the substance into the air, the air becomes more and more charged with moisture, takes up the water from the substance more and more slowly, until at length it becomes saturated and will hold no more. Then

Small tanks for experimental lots of grain.

Paris and London Photo Agency.

drying ceases.   If we wish the drying process to continue, we must either substitute a new portion of dry air, or we must extract the moisture from the air to enable it to take up more.   Both methods are effectual in practice.   In practice it is found that a current of air—that is to say, the constant renewal of the moist air—dries a substance much more rapidly than stagnant air ; and in practice it is found that even stagnant air will dry a substance completely if we furnish the air with some hygroscopic substance, such as chloride of zinc, or sulphuric acid, which will extract the moisture from the air as fast as it enters the air.

But there is another way of drying the air besides extracting the moisture from it. Warm air will hold more moisture than cold air, and the hotter the air, the more moisture it will hold ; so that hot air, even though it actually contain more moisture than cold air, may be relatively drier, and able to absorb more moisture.   Hence the best possible condition for drying is a current of hot air.

Paris and London Photo Agency.

Wheat grown by Mr Roseveare, Gains Cross Farm, Blandford Electrified on the left, unelectrified on the right. The straw grown from electrified seed is stouter, and the ears are longer and plumper.

Heat has yet a further effect in aiding the process of drying, though by itself it is, as we have seen, useless. It increases the activity of the particles of moisture in the damp substance, and helps them to fly off from its surface into the surrounding air. Hence we arrive at the optimum conditions for drying, and find that drying will take place most rapidly when the body to be dried is placed in the most rapid current of the hottest air.

In the case of seed grain, very hot air must not be used, for above a certain temperature the grain is killed. We must therefore depend mainly upon the rapidity with which the air can be changed, and let this air be of the maximum permissible temperature, which is about 100 degrees F.

After the electrification of the seed is completed, therefore, the next process is to raise the seed out of the soaking tank, preferably in baskets, so that the surface moisture may drain away, and then to deposit it in an apparatus in which it is subjected to a blast of air at 100 degrees F., either driven or drawn through the mass of seed, until it is dried to the proper degree of desiccation.   One effect of the war has been to diminish very much the quantity of beer that has been brewed, and the consequence of this has been that a large number of malt-kilns have been put out of use. Many of these have been utilised for the purpose of drying electrified seed, and have answered the purpose very well.   Owing to the shortage of every kind of labour, however, it has not always been possible to engage the services of skilled maltsters ; and a malt-kiln requires skilled supervision. Thus it has happened that in some cases the seed has not been properly dried, and some failures are attributable to this cause. Fortunately, the cause is no longer in operation, and no further accidents of this kind need be anticipated.

The process is now complete, and the seed may be sown.   It should be sown promptly, for the effect of the electrification

Paris and London Photo Agency

A corner of Mr Fry's laboratory.

is not permanent.   Under ordinary circumstances, and if the seed is kept meanwhile in a dry place, the effect lasts for about a month.   It has upon occasion lasted for considerably longer, but it cannot be depended on to do so, and it is unsafe to defer the sowing for more than a month.   After this period, though some effect may be obtained, the full effect will not be obtained, and the trouble and expense will be to some extent wasted.

CHAPTER III

RESULTS

THE electrification of seed improves in many ways the crop grown from it. In most cases it improves the crop in those ways that are commercially desirable ; but in a few cases it has produced a result that, while increasing the quantity of the crop, has increased it in a way that is commercially undesirable. For example, the quantitative yield of tobacco leaf has been much increased ; but, in fine tobacco, what is wanted is not so much increase in bulk as improvement in quality. A smaller leaf of better quality is of more value commercially than a huge rank leaf. The result actually produced has been the latter—a much larger leaf, but of inferior quality. It is by no means necessary or inevitable, however, that the result should be of this character. It must be remembered that, with all seeds but those of cereals, the process is in its infancy, and we are far yet from knowing all its possibilities.

In this connection, a recent experiment on peas is highly significant. Leguminous plants of all kinds are refractory to the process, which has hitherto produced little result upon any of them. They have therefore been electrified in various ways and in various solutions, and the effect of one of these experiments on pea Duke of Albany was very remarkable. Duke of Albany is a pea that grows to a height of about four feet, and in light soil has rather light-coloured foliage, the leaves being about two inches in diameter. In the experiment in question, a row of fifteen yards in length was sown, as to one half, with peas electrified in a certain manner, while the other half was sown with untreated peas out of the same bag as a control. The control seeds all grew as

Small experimental tank at Godmanstone Farm. Mr W. F. Smith, farm bailiff, with two trusses of barley (on the left) grown from treated seed, and two (on the right) from untreated. Note the longer straw and deeper colour of the electrified sample.

normal Duke of Albany's, of the usual
height, colour, and size of leaf. The electrified peas threw up plants that grew to
only about eighteen inches in height, were
of a very dark green colour, and their
leaves were no larger than half-crowns.
The pods were about the usual size, and
contained the usual number of peas, but
were of much darker colour than those of
the controls. Now peas, garden peas at
any rate, are grown solely for their seeds,
and, except in colour, the seeds of the
treated plants were not very different from
those of the controls ; but if the peas had
been grown as some plants — coleus, for
instance — are, for depth of colour, they
would have taken a prize at any show ;
and if they had been grown for the flavour
of their foliage, as tested either by eating
or by smoking, it can scarcely be supposed
that this flavour would not have been
altered, and enhanced. It seems, therefore,
that, by modifying the electric treatment
of the seed, we can to some extent guide

the resulting alteration of the crop in the direction we desire.

All this, however, is matter for future experiment, and will take years to determine. At present the potentialities of the process have been determined only for wheat, oats, and barley, and even for these probably only in part. In them, however, it has been wholly beneficial, and has resulted in increasing the yield in just those respects that are economically desirable.

In the first place, the quantity or bulk of the grain is increased, and is usually increased to a very material extent ; in the second place, the quality of the grain is improved ; and in the third place, the straw is increased in length, in weight, and in stoutness. All these results are commercially valuable, and it would be very desirable, if it were practicable, to give in figures, in bushel measures, in pounds and hundred-weight avoirdupois, and in percentages, the advantage in yield of the crops from electrified seed over the crops from seed that has not been electrified. It would seem to the uninstructed that this must be a very easy thing to do, and that, out of the hundreds of cases in which electrified seed has been grown by farmers for profit, some scores at least of weighed and measured results should be available for citation. But those who form such an anticipation know little of the nature of the farmer, and, as the scarcity of weighed and measured results must tell against the right estimation of the process, it may be as well to explain here the kind of man the farmer is, so as to account for this scarcity. A mere mention or a brief explanation will look like an excuse; and this is no excuse. It is a good, sound, valid reason.

Farmers are notoriously a conservative race, slow to adopt new ideas, new processes, new implements, and new materials; and there is good reason for their conservatism. Agriculture is the oldest of all industries, and one of the most complex and difficult to master and to pursue with success. It is so much at the mercy of the capricious forces of nature that it is impossible for even the ablest farmer to pursue it with constant success. Farming requires more intelligence than any other industrial occupation, the reasons being two. In the first place, the farmer's task is with living things, which are indefinitely more difficult to mould to his purposes than are the inanimate materials dealt with by the engineer, the miner, the ironmaster, the textile worker, the builder, or the cabinet-maker. In the second place, the operations that he must conduct are much more numerous and diverse than need to be pursued by one man in any other industry. The operator in a factory may pass a life-time in doing nothing else but fashioning the heads of pins, or attending to the regular movements of a group of spindles or looms. Such operations call for little skill, little intelligence, and that all of one kind, and a very limited kind ; but the agricultural labourer's duties vary with every day in the year, and every hour in the day. He must " plough and sow, and reap and mow, and be a farmer's boy." His work is with living things ; and living things, whether animal or vegetable, cannot be managed by coercion. They must be humoured. They must be understood. They must be studied individually. Unlike inanimate substances, they have their likes and dislikes. Unlike inanimate substances, they are subject to competition, both from one another and from other live things. The plants of wheat in a wheat-field have rivals in one another, and a competitor in every weed that grows near them ; and the live stock similarly compete with one another—aye, and sometimes bully one another, so that one will monopolise the best pasture, and another will be left to get what he can. The living things by which the farmer makes his livelihood are subject to diseases, many of them infectious ; must be increased by reproduction, a mysterious process ; are subject to laws of heredity but little understood; and throughout the whole of his operations the farmer finds himself everywhere confronted with mystery. In such circumstances it behoves him to walk warily, and to think twice before he leaves the old ways, trodden smooth by the feet of innumerable predecessors, and therefore tried and safe. They may not lead to astonishing and dramatic success, but at least they are sure not to lead to dire disaster; so he goes in the old ways. Besides this, the farmer is of necessity keenly observant. His whole livelihood depends daily and hourly on the keenness and faithfulness of his observation of a thousand things that the townsman is utterly blind to. At an agricultural show, a townsman can see no difference between the winner of the champion cup and the beast that is but commended; but to every farmer present they are wide as the poles asunder. The farmer is keenly observant, and has a tenacious memory. Both are necessary in his business; and the farmer is not slow to observe the blunders committed by his would-be teachers, and not quick to forget them. No class of men in the world is so prone to mistrust the amateur; and it must in justice be said that no class of men in the world has better reason. Among amateurs, the professional farmer reckons the professor of agriculture, whose experiments are regarded with disdain, and whose advice is received with sceptical indifference; and in this again the farmer is not without justification. An instance will suffice.

Professors used to make merry over a queer superstition entertained by farmers that there was a strong connection between the disease of wheat known as rust, and the presence of barberry bushes in the hedges of the wheat-field. Rust, they said, appears on wheat, if not solely where there are barberries in the hedges, yet much more frequently in such fields, which are also subject to more virulent attacks. Over this " irrational superstition" the professors made merry, until it was found that rust is a fungus; that, like many fungi, it passes through different stages in its existence; and that one of these stages is passed upon the barberry. When this discovery was made, it was the farmers' turn to laugh, and it gave them a pull upon the professors, and a distrust of their judgment, which remain to this day; for farmers not only are keen observers, as the incident shows, but also have tenacious memories.

In comparison with the town-dweller, the farmer leads a solitary life. His neighbours are few, and are comparatively far away; and, having fewer opportunities of human intercourse, he has fewer gifts of expression. He feels his way to his modes of action by dint of accumulated experiences, and reasonings that he never puts into words, so that he seems to reach his decisions by a sort of instinct; but his decisions are usually right, and founded on good reason, though he may be unable to put his reasons into words. He shares with other professional men a

contempt for the amateur and for the outsider who offers advice, and perhaps he feels
this contempt more than men of other
professions, and this for two reasons. He
feels more than men of other professions
the vital necessity of experience, and the
uselessness of instruction that is not accompanied by experience; and he has, in
that tenacious memory of his, not a few
instances in which the advice of outsiders
has proved to be wrong. He has seen
the amateur and inexperienced agriculturist
suffer heavy loss by the premature adoption
of methods that have been insufficiently
tried; and thus he acquires a distrust of
all new methods—a distrust that he is apt
to carry too far.

For these reasons it was not easy to induce
farmers to try the method of submitting
their seeds to the electro-chemical process.
It was new, it was strange, and it was
recommended by an outsider who was not
a farmer, and had no experience of agriculture; but, under a certain amount of pressure

from his employer, a farmer was at last prevailed upon to try it. He tried it, but he tried it with a firm and settled conviction that it was useless and would turn out to be a failure. It is not too much to say, for he has himself admitted, that he wanted it to be a failure, and therefore he made no effort to make it succeed. But much to his surprise it did succeed. Its success was undeniable, and upon a second trial he was less sceptical and more inclined to give a fair chance to the new process. Again it was successful, and now he pursued it in good earnest. He put up a plant to treat his own seed under the supervision of the inventor, and is now become an enthusiastic advocate of the new process.

Farmers pay little attention to the advice of inexperienced outsiders, and their reluctance is natural, and is usually not unwise; but they pay much attention to the experience of other farmers, and are always willing to try a method that has been found successful by their neighbours. Farmers meet at markets and at ordinaries and talk over farming affairs, and in this way a knowledge of the electro-chemical process and the practice of employing it spread from farm to farm in the neighbourhood in which it was invented and first employed. For several years this was the only way in which it spread, for the inventor himself is as cautious as a farmer, and was unwilling to make his invention publicly known until it was proved and proved and better proved, until it was proved up to the hilt and could not be gainsaid. This stage is now reached, and he has been induced at length, under some little pressure, to make it known to the world.

But now arose a difficulty from the general practice of farmers. It has been said that, owing to the circumstances of their lives, they have little gift of expression. Their lives are passed out of doors, in actual contact with things, and it is irksome to them to sit down, after an exhausting day's work in the open air, and commit their thoughts to paper. Their memories serve them well enough, and they see no necessity to call in the aid of pen and paper to assist them. For this reason farmers are not good book-keepers. They keep in their minds general results rather than accurate figures, for which they see no necessity, and which consume time and energy that, as it seems to the farmer, would be better employed in other work. If he sees, as he is quick to see, that a certain manure or a certain mode of cultivation produces a material increase in his crop, that is enough for him. He sees no necessity to weigh and measure the result to determine precisely how many pounds or bushels he has gained. He is a busy man. He is always short of labour. Weighing and measuring on the large scale required by farm crops are tedious processes, and consume much labour and time, often at the busiest season of the year. It is only during the last four years, the years of war, when labour has been scarce almost to the point of famine, that the electro-chemical process has been used by farmers ; and it is only in a very small fraction of the cases in which it has been used that weighed and measured results have been obtained. Even of these, a considerable proportion would not have been obtained if an independent expert, quite unconnected with the farmers, had not been sent by the Board of Agriculture to visit several farms for the express purpose of investigating the results of the process, and had not himself measured off portions of the crops with scientific accuracy, reaped them, threshed them, and weighed and measured the proceeds. General impressions of the value of the process, opinions in its favour, descriptions of the superiority of the crops resulting from it, the inventor has in plenty ; but weighed and measured results are few. As far as they go, however, they are almost uniformly in favour of the process ; and when we take into account the inevitable uncertainty and apparent caprice of the results of farming operations, when we allow for the disturbing influences, some of which will be enumerated on a subsequent page, the general uniformity of benefit that has resulted from the use of the process is such as to establish its value beyond the shadow of a doubt.

In previous years failures were mingled with successes. As seasons went by, and as with each season the process was better understood and its details perfected, the proportion of successes to failures increased. The reasons of the failures were discovered and provided against, until in the harvest of 1918 failures—by which is meant failure to secure a more valuable crop from the treated than from the untreated seed—were almost entirely eliminated.

The following are the measured and weighed results reported up to the present as obtained in the harvest of 1918 :—

[TABLE

	Gain per Acre in Grain.	Gain per Acre in Straw.
1. Mr W. W. Lovelace, Puddlehinton, Dorchester.	Wheat, 7 bushels.	2 tons 8 cwt.
2. Mr C. Foot, Bincombe, Dorchester.	Wheat, 6½ bushels.	*Loss* 1 cwt.
3. Mr H. H. Cake, Bincombe, Dorchester.	Barley, 16 bushels.	Gain 9 cwt.
4. Mr H. Legg, Blashenwell, Corfe Castle.	Oats, 18 bushels.	Gain 10 cwt.
5. Mr W. W. Lovelace, Puddlehinton.	Oats, 6 bushels.	Gain 4 cwt.
6. Messrs S. & H. Smith, Rollington, Corfe Castle.	Oats, 19 bushels.	*Loss* 5 cwt.
7. Mrs Duke, Godmanstone.	Barley, 2 bushels *loss*.	Gain about 33 per cent.*

* The straw was estimated by the farmer when the whole field was threshed.

These results were obtained by the independent expert already mentioned. In addition, the following have been reported by the farmers concerned :—

	Gain per Acre in Grain.	Gain per Acre in Straw.
8. Mr S. Hawkins, Whitestone, Exeter.	Wheat, 8¼ bushels.	
9. Mrs Duke, Godmanstone.	Wheat, 7¼ bushels.	
10. Mr A. H. Moore, Woodlands Park, Leatherhead.	Wheat, 5¾ bushels.	
11. Mr Godwin, Moreton, Dorset.	Oats, 12 bushels.	
12. Mr R. S. Hicks, Wilbraham Temple, Cambs.	Oats, 5 bushels.	
13. Mr Stidson, Thurleston, Devon.	Barley, 50 per cent.	
14. Mr W. T. Maye, Charlton, Dorset.	Barley, 21 per cent.	
15. Mr A. T. Cock, Ford Farm, Lispeard.	Wheat, 12 bushels.	20 per cent.
16. R. S. Hicks, Esq., Wilbraham Temple, Cambs.	Mangels, 2 tons 15 cwt.	

It is true that this is but a meagre list in comparison with the 150 farmers who reaped last year corn grown from seed treated by the Wolfryn process, but the reasons for the scarcity of measured and weighed results have already been given ; and these reports have been supplemented by a chorus of approval, expressed in general terms, which it is scarcely worth while to reproduce. It may be mentioned, however, that of 27 farmers supplied by Messrs Holman & Sons in this, their first season, every one has reported that his yield of grain was much larger from the treated than from the untreated seed, but that, owing to scarcity of labour, he was unable to give weighed and measured results.

Through other electrifying stations the inventor has received fewer reports from farmers ; but he is not disheartened by this. It is no libel on farmers to say that, if the results had been unsatisfactory, the agents who electrified the seed, and were paid for doing so, would certainly have heard of it. In this case, at any rate, no news is good news. It would not be true to say that no complaints have been received. There have been a very few ; but in every case, without any exception, in which the result has been disappointing, it was found on investigation that a manifest error had been made in the application of the process. Either the operator was inexperienced and misunderstood his instructions, or there was some oversight, or some fault in the apparatus. In the most efficient factories mistakes are made. The best workmen sometimes spoil their work ; and, though the process of electrifying seeds is a very simple process, men are fallible and will sometimes make mistakes ; apparatus is of human construction and will sometimes break down or get out of order — and then things will go wrong ; but *in no case has failure been traced to the process itself.* Whenever there has been a failure—and, since the process is carried out by human agency, there have been a few—the failure has without exception been traced to faulty execution.

Of the fourteen results of growing electrified corn that are given above, one-half were obtained by an official who investigated the matter on behalf of the Food Production Department of the Board of Agriculture. This gentleman spent about a fortnight over his investigations among the farms of Dorsetshire on which electrified seed was growing alongside of unelectrified seed from the same bulk. His method was to measure off two plots of two perches each, one plot on each side of the dividing line between the two crops. The two plots were so close together as to minimise any chance of difference in the character of the soil on which they were grown (see pp. 77 *et seq.*), and all the farmers agreed that there was practically no difference. Each plot was reaped as close as possible to the ground, and the resulting crop was then carefully threshed, weighed, and measured. About these results, therefore, there can be no possible doubt ; and it is noticeable that six out of the seven showed a positive advantage in favour of the electrified seed, and the average advantage was very considerable. Of the seventh case, in which no advantage appeared, I shall have something to say later on.

The official made his report to the Food Production Department, but this report has not yet been published, and presumably will not now be published ; but the Department has composed the following Memorandum, which it issues to members of the public who inquire as to the merits of the Wolfryn process :—

Food Production Department—Technical Committee.

Wolfryn Electro-Chemical Treatment of Seeds.

This process is understood to consist in passing a regulated electric current through a tank containing a weak solution of some neutral salt, such as common salt, in which the seed undergoing treatment is steeped.

Pot experiments with treated barley and oats made at the Rothamsted Experimental Station in 1918, at the request of the Technical Committee, gave a result slightly in favour of the treatment in the case of oats, but negative in the case of barley.

The process has gained some popularity among farmers, particularly in Dorsetshire ; in the latter county it is stated that over 2000 acres were under treated crops in 1918. A member of the Technical Committee, accompanied by the Executive Officer of the Dorsetshire Agricultural Executive Committee, visited certain crops and reported that on the date of inspection (July 18th) the treated crops in most cases appeared to give the heavier yields. This view was supported by actual weighings of small areas of certain of the crops made later on behalf of the Committee. The weighings showed an increased yield of corn in six out of seven cases (wheat, barley, and oats) varying from 240–900 lbs. per acre, and a decrease in the seventh case (barley). Potatoes gave a decreased yield in four cases out of the five selected.

In interpreting these results it must be remembered that the weighings were made on small plots, that the plots were not in duplicate, and that, as far as the Committee are aware, no special steps were taken to secure uniformity in the soil on which the trials were made.

On the information at their disposal the Committee are not in a position to come to any definite conclusion on the claims put forward for the process ; but, assuming that the treatment does actually increase the yield of the resulting crops, it would still be impossible to say at present whether such results were due to the treatment as a whole, including the effect of the electric current, or whether equally good results might not be obtained by either soaking the grain in the appropriate fluid (or water) for a suitable period with subsequent drying, or by drying the grain at a suitable temperature without the previous soaking or electrical treatment. Experiments are in progress with a view to securing information on these points.

TECHNICAL COMMITTEE,
FOOD PRODUCTION DEPARTMENT,
72 VICTORIA STREET, S.W. 1.

It will be seen that the Memorandum contains a certain amount of fact, but this is enveloped in so much commentary that the facts are obscured, to some extent thrust out of sight, and to some extent minimised and depreciated. If we strip away this commentary and allow the facts to stand by themselves, they are as follows:—

In six cases out of seven, the crops from the electrified seed showed an important advantage over the crops from unelectrified seed.

The amount of the advantage ranged from 240 lbs. to 900 lbs. of grain per acre; or from 5 bushels 20 lbs. to 16 bushels 4 lbs. per acre; or from 8 per cent. to 61 per cent.

The average gain in yield of grain was 10½ bushels, or more than 2½ sacks per acre.

The money value of this increase is, at present prices, from £2, 4s. 3d. to £7, 12s. per acre, with an average profit of £4, 16s. after deducting the cost of electrification.

These are the facts as ascertained, recorded, and published by the Board of Agriculture, and the facts need no commentary.

But the explanations, surmises, and doubts by which the facts are overlaid and obscured do need some commentary ; and the comments that I venture to make upon them are these :—

When divested of unnecessary verbiage and put in plain terms, the comments of the Board of Agriculture, or of its Food Production Department, or of the Technical

Committee of that Department, whichever is the author of them, amount to this :

1. The Board, or the Department, or the Committee, is not sure that the conditions under which the treated and untreated crops were growing were identical.

2. The Board is not sure that the differences between the crops may not have been due to some other cause than the electrification of the seed.

3. Though this important advantage followed in six cases out of seven when electrified and unelectrified seeds were sown side by side on large acreages under ordinary farming conditions, yet some experiments in pots showed no important advantage.

Let us take these comments seriatim.

1. The electrified and unelectrified seeds grew side by side in the same field on adjoining patches or plots of ground ; but the Board is not sure that the conditions under which the two crops were grown were identical. Reference to p. 77 *et seq.* will show what the Board probably had in mind

in making this comment, and it must be admitted at once that the conditions were not identical. If we are to be scientifically accurate, conditions that are identical in the strict sense of the word can never be secured. Even in laboratory experiments, when the experimenter has everything under strict control, and can use not only seed from the same bulk, as was used in these field experiments, but also soil from the same compost heap, and pots from the same cast, and can stand them side by side, and treat them to the best of his knowledge and skill in precisely the same manner, measuring and weighing every drop of water and every grain of manure that is supplied to them— even in these conditions the treatment of the two plants is not identical. The conditions may, by additional precautions, be made more and more closely alike ; but they can never be identical, and to complain that they are not identical is not to the point. They must be different : that is unavoidable ; but the point is, *were they sufficiently different to account for the differences in the crops?* This is all that matters, and, as to this, the officer of the Board who made the experiments must be presumed to know his business. He was sent to make the fairest possible comparison, and there is no reason to suppose that he was lacking in skill or in honesty. Both he and the farmers upon whose land the crops were growing were convinced that there was no such difference in the soil or aspect or other conditions of the plots compared as would account for the difference in the crops. The cause of this difference must therefore have been in the difference of the seed.

2. Supposing and granting, however, that the difference in the crops is due to difference in the seed, the Board is not sure that the difference in the seed is due to its electrification. It may have been due to the soaking. It may have been due to the soaking combined with the drying. Or it may have been due to the soaking in a chemical solution.

These surmises have a certain plausibility, and are in accordance with our knowledge of the subject. It is known to every gardener that seed will germinate more rapidly if it is soaked for a few hours before it is sown. The germination is usually accelerated by several days. It is known to every experienced and advanced agriculturist that soaking and then drying the seed equalises and improves the germination, though not the germinating energy. These things have been known since the time of the Pharaohs, and, though it cannot be positively asserted, it is probable that our first parents, when they were cultivating the Garden of Eden, soaked their seed in the waters of the Tigris or the Euphrates. Soaking the seed in order to accelerate germination is one of the routine operations of gardening ; but if the Board of Agriculture wishes to test the value of the practice, no harm will be done by its experiments on the subject. It is always desirable to test the truth of traditional beliefs, and the Board might add to these experiments others designed to ascertain whether a stone thrown into the air really does, as is generally believed, fall to the ground.

The effect on the crop of soaking and drying the seed was tested some forty years ago with German laboriousness by two German experimenters, and the Board of Agriculture has unearthed these forgotten experiments and republished them in its Journal for February 1919. The experiments, it is to be remarked, were made on no cereal but rye. Considerable increase in the crop was noted in some cases ; but the gist and moral of the experiments—a moral which the Board of Agriculture fails to point—is that, although these experiments were made forty years ago, and although they were made in Germany, from whence all scientific and reliable knowledge has been supposed for so many years to emanate, the practice they inculcate has never been adopted, even in Germany. If there had been any value in it, sufficient to compensate for the trouble required, we may be sure that it would have become general long ago.

The Board of Agriculture is now, it appears, conducting experiments to discover whether the increase in the crop, which the Board does not deny, may not be due to the soaking in the chemical solution, and not to the accompanying electrification. If the Board had communicated with Mr Fry, he could have enlightened it, and saved it the trouble of experimenting. The possibility of the effect being due to the soaking in the chemical and not to the electrification is obvious, so obvious that the Board of Agriculture noticed it at once, and it is needless to say that it was present to the mind of the inventor of the Wolfryn process from the very outset of his experiments. He has found—and the information is very much at the service of the Board of Agriculture—that soaking in a chemical solution and subsequent drying of the seed does produce some increase in the resulting crop ; and the increase is sometimes so considerable that it seemed worth while to take out a patent for the operation. Mr Fry accordingly applied for and obtained a patent, and the belated experiments of the Board of Agriculture will be an infringement of this patent—an infringement that Mr Fry is not likely, however, to resent; and for this reason: that, though in many cases an improvement in the crop does undoubtedly follow on the practice, yet this improvement is usually far less than is obtained by the additional use of electricity; and when once the seed is soaked in the chemical solution, and must thereafter be dried, by far the greater part of the trouble and expense is already incurred, and the additional cost of electrifying is so small, and the additional gain so great, that, having gone thus far, it would be silly not to complete the process.

The only other matter that calls for comment in the Board of Agriculture's Memorandum is that referring to potatoes. The electrified potatoes showed a decreased yield in four cases out of the five selected.

In fairness to the inventor and to his process, it should have been added that he has never advised its adoption for potatoes except experimentally. It is obvious that potatoes are very different from wheat, oats, and barley, and that the former require treatment very different from the latter. The treatment of potatoes is still in the experimental stage ; the plots selected by the Board's expert were experimental ; and a certain proportion of experiments are, as will be presently explained, bound to fail, and intended to fail. Great success has followed the electrification of seed potatoes in some instances ; considerable loss has followed in others. This is the history of all such experiments, and will be the history of all subsequent experiments. It is by the method of trial and error that success is at last attained ; and during the experimental stage, in which potatoes still are, failure is as much to be expected as success. To take one feature only : it is manifest that potatoes contain a very much larger proportion of water than corn, and if potatoes are dried to the same degree as corn is dried, that is, until all the water but about 12 per cent. of the weight of the substance is extracted, the potatoes will be seriously damaged, and may even be killed. This is, of course, always taken into consideration by the inventor himself, but it has not always been remembered by those who have electrified comparatively large quantities ; and the seed potatoes, and consequently the crops, have suffered in consequence. It would be manifestly unfair and misleading to put such failures down to the discredit of the Wolfryn process. This process is not yet recommended, and has not been recommended, for potatoes except experimentally. Some of the experiments have been very successful, and there is no reason to doubt that, when the conditions of treatment have been accurately determined, potato crops will be as much benefited as crops of grain.

CHAPTER IV

FAILURES

DURING the early stages of experimentation on any given kind of seed, and, indeed, during the early stages of experimentation on almost anything, failures are inevitable, and are normal. The purpose in view is to discover the best method, and the best method cannot be selected if all are alike. What are to be discovered are the limits within which the best treatment lies ; and these limits can only be discovered by going beyond them, and so courting failure. For instance, it is desired to find the best duration of treatment for a kind of seed that has not been tried before. A large number of parcels of the seed are taken, and are treated for different lengths of time, beginning with a period that is pretty sure to be too short, and ending with one that is pretty sure to be too long. Each lot of seed is then sown, and, if the guess as to the proper duration has been about right, those seeds that have had the shortest treatment will show no advantage, and with them the process may be said to have failed ; and those seeds that have had the longest treatment will have been injured, and perhaps will not germinate at all, and with them also the process may be said, in a certain sense, to have failed. In one sense, then, the experiments with the first and last lots will be failures ; but manifestly this is a wrong term to apply to them. The purpose of the experiment is not to produce an increase in the crop yielded by every lot, but to find out which lot yields the greatest increase. In this purpose the experiment will be so far successful that it will justify further trials in which the extremes are omitted, and the new lots begun with a longer treatment than the shortest of the previous trial, and ended with a shorter treatment than the longest of that trial; and so by repeated trials the duration is narrowed down until it can be fixed within half an hour or so. Then the degree of concentration or strength of the solution is tested in a similar way; and again, in this series of tests, some of the lots will exhibit no effect, and others will be damaged or killed; but it would be a misnomer to call either of them failures.

When once the standard treatment for any kind of seed is determined, no failure is met with in laboratory experiments, provided the subsequent experiments are properly conducted; but failures may still be met with in field experiments, or in the practical experience of farmers, even if the process is properly carried out. Such failures, in which no increase, or perhaps an actual diminution, of the yield of the treated seed is discovered on threshing the crop, are rare, but they do occur now and then, and they must be expected and allowed for. The causes are various, and are sometimes assignable and sometimes not.

It must be remembered that the raising of agricultural crops is an extremely complex operation, subject to conditions that are imperfectly understood, and that, when electricity is not used, crops sometimes fail for reasons quite apart from any defect in the quality of the seed. The depredations of rabbits, hares, birds, insects, and fungous diseases are by no means uniformly spread over a large field. The damage inflicted by rabbits will be greatest on the side nearest to their warren. The damage inflicted by pheasants will be greater on the side nearest to the wood in which they roost. The competition of weeds will be in the parts of the field nearest to the hedgerows, and some forms of fungous disease spread from the hedgerows in which the fungi pass one phase of their existence. Again, some weeds, such as couch, occur in patches, and these patches may be larger, or more numerous, or both, in one part of a field than in another. In some fields the soil is patchy, gravel coming to the surface in places and being absent elsewhere ; or the subsoil may be different or may come nearer to the surface in one place than in another, so that here there may be a couple of feet of good loam, and there only six inches. Again, if a field is on a slope, the surface rain-water will flow from the higher to the lower level ; and if the subsoil slopes and is impervious, the rain that has soaked into the soil will have a similar trend. Even if the subsoil is not impervious, water that soaks into the soil will spread horizontally, and, if the field is on a slope, will come to the surface and flow down. But rain-water in the soil dissolves the manurial substances in the soil, and carries them with it ; and when the rain evaporates and the soil dries, the manurial substances are left where the rain has carried them to. For this reason, the lower portion of a sloping field is richer in manure than the upper portion, and, other things being equal, will yield a better crop. So, too, the lower portion of a field is less exposed to certain winds than the upper portion, and these have their influence on the quantity of the crop produced. The trees in the hedgerows rob the adjacent parts of the field of a portion of their nourishment, shade them from the sun, and protect them from certain winds. Sheep may have been folded upon one part of the field and not upon another, so producing a great difference in fertility ; and even where they are folded they manure the ground irregularly. From all these considerations it will be seen that the crop in one part of a field is by no means necessarily grown under the same conditions as the crop in another part of the same field ; but, on the contrary, and especially if the field is large, or sloping, or both, part of the crop is almost necessarily grown under more favourable conditions than other parts, and uniformity in the conditions of growth must be rather the exception than the rule. The differences between one part of a field and another may not be great, but, as the crop is subjected to these conditions week after week and month after month, they must have their effect, and must to some extent vitiate the comparison between crops grown in different parts of the same field.

So potent are these influences that they must be allowed for, and are allowed for, in estimating the value of any application of treatment to the crop. Of all artificial or chemical manures, none has more thoroughly established its value and reputation among farmers than sulphate of ammonia. It is used in immense quantities all over the country, and no agriculturist ever dreams of questioning its value. But sulphate of ammonia is by no means uniformly successful in increasing the crop. It usually produces a very decided increase, but it does not always produce the same amount of increase, and sometimes it produces no increase at all. Sometimes the crop manured with sulphate of ammonia is a failure. But as it is successful in increasing the crop in about 80 per cent. of the cases in which it is used, it is recognised, in spite of its failure in the remaining 20 per cent., as one of the most valuable manures that is used on the farm. When we speak of the electro-chemical treatment of seed as being a valuable adjunct to agriculture, and as a powerful means of increasing the crops, we must therefore not be understood to assert that it will be successful in every case, or that the increase that it usually produces will be of the same amount in every case. If we can show that it is followed by a decided increase in the yield in 80 per cent. of the cases in which it is tried, we have proved our point. Up to the present, it has produced a decided increase in much more than 80 per cent. of the cases in which it has been tried.

In the circumstances above described, there may be an apparent failure, but there will not be a real failure. There is no real failure unless the treated seed, when sown and grown in similar soil and under the same conditions as the untreated, fails to show a substantial increase in yield. We

6

now consider the cases in which there is a real failure, and the causes of it.

In the early stages of applying a new and ill-understood process, failures are inevitable. Even when a process is well known and fully established by the successful practice of years, there are occasional failures. As we all know, even the electric light sometimes goes out suddenly : even the telephone sometimes fails to carry its messages : even a locomotive engine sometimes breaks an axle or a connecting-rod : even an explosive shell may be a dud. Perfection is seldom maintained continuously in human affairs, and even the electro-chemical treatment of seeds sometimes fails to produce an increase in the resulting crop as compared with the control. To condemn the process on this account would be unreasonable. It would be as unreasonable as to refuse to travel by railway because there is sometimes an accident on the line. To refrain from using the process because the increase in the crop is not always up to the usual mark is as unreasonable as to refuse to travel by railway because trains are not always up to time. " Depend upon it," says Dr Johnson, " a fallible being will fail somewhere"; and depend upon it, a process executed by fallible beings will fail sometimes.

The reasons for some of these failures have already been given. They lie in the unevenness and irregularity of the soil and other conditions in which the seed is sown. The reasons for other failures, or partial failures, lie in the faulty performance of the process. If the process is wrongly performed, its failure lies at the door of the performer, not at that of the process. We might as well blame the engine for not going when the fire is not lit or the steam is not turned on, or the clock for stopping when it is not wound. In the early experiments, mistakes were made by the inventor himself. That was inevitable. He had to find out by the expensive process of trial and error the conditions of success. These conditions are now ascertained for cereals, and now there should be no failures; but the mischief is that amateurs will attempt to conduct a process with which they are imperfectly acquainted, in which they omit some necessary precaution, and then, when failure results, they blame, not themselves, but the process.

In the early days of the experiments, the inventor freely distributed treated seed to various people for trial. As he had not then ascertained all the necessary precautions, some of these lots were faulty, and resulted in failure. The experimenters thereupon condemned the seed, and the process, and the inventor, and would have no more to do with any of them. The attitude was perhaps not unnatural, and it may have been incautious on the part of the inventor to distribute the seed before he was sure of success; but, if incautious in this respect, he is cautious as an experimenter, and wished to eliminate the personal factor. However careful he may be, an inventor can scarcely be sure that he does not unintentionally and unconsciously favour his own invention, and Mr Fry desired to eliminate every possible source of uncertainty. He therefore sent samples of treated and untreated seed to certain agricultural colleges, with the request that they might be grown experimentally. This was in the early days of the process, when the proper conditions were only guessed at, and when failures were frequent ; and the particular experiments in question were failures. They either showed an actual loss, or no gain, or a gain so small as to be within the normal margin of error. In the light of subsequent experience it is now known that, with seed treated as these samples were treated, no benefit could be expected ; but the colleges to which the seeds were sent did not take the view that the tests they were asked to make were experimental. They regarded them as decisive of the value of the process ; and as the results showed no benefit, they condemned the process wholly and utterly, and regard this condemnation as final.

Of course it is to be remembered that the inventor of the Wolfryn process is not a professor. He is not even an agriculturist. He is an outsider, and professional men do not welcome the intrusion of an outsider into their domain, which they are apt to guard with a jealous exclusiveness. Doctors are not enthusiastic admirers of the successes of the bone-setter ; military men have not much respect for the amateur strategist ; the clergy are impatient of the theologian who has not gone through the orthodox theological training ; and professors of agriculture are not wholly exempt from the common failings of humanity.

It is quite true that this attitude of the professional man to the amateur is in most cases justified. A little knowledge, if it is expressed with airs of importance, is very apt to expose its possessor to ridicule ; but it is not always safe to despise the outsider. Many of the most important inventions, which have completely revolutionised various departments of industry, have been made by outsiders, men trained and brought up in occupations with which their inventions had nothing at all to do. It is well known that Arkwright, a barber, invented the spinning jenny ; that Newcomen, an ironmonger, and Watt, a mathematical instrument maker, between them invented the steam engine ; and that Trevithick, a miner, and George Stephenson, another miner, between them invented the steam locomotive ; that Dollond, a weaver, and Hall, a barrister, both invented achromatic lenses ; that Lassels, a brewer, discovered the satellites of Uranus, which had itself been discovered by W. Herschel, a music-master ; that Graham, who discovered the diurnal variation of the compass, was a clock-maker ; and that the gravity escapement in clocks was invented by Becket-Denison, who was a barrister ; that the electric telegraph was perfected by Wheatstone, a maker of musical instruments ;—and the list might be extended indefinitely. There is therefore no *primâ facie* improbability in the invention by Mr

Fry, who is not an agriculturist, of an important improvement in agriculture. It may be that the professors of agriculture are not very pleased that an outsider should have discovered an important aid that they have overlooked to agriculture, and they have not hitherto shown themselves sympathetic towards the process; but the field of experimentation that it opens up is so vast that there is plenty of room for an army of experimenters.

But even now that the process is, if not perfected, yet practically quite ascertained and successful, failures do occasionally occur; and when they occur, it is invariably found upon investigation that the fault has been, not in the process itself, but in lapses from it. The most important of these are the following :—

1. The solution employed may not be ideally suitable to the soil in which the seed is grown. There is much need of further research in this respect. Seed that has been treated electro-chemically may show an im-

portant gain over untreated seed when the two are sown in one soil, and yet, when other seed of the same batch is sown in another soil, there may be no material difference. It is evident that the determining factor must be the suitability of the salt used in the solution to the soil in which the seed is grown.

2. The duration of the process may not be suitable to the kind of seed under treatment. A period of treatment that is right for one kind of seed may be enough to electrocute another kind, and injure or destroy its germinating energy. A duration of treatment that may be right for one kind of seed may not be long enough to produce any appreciable effect upon another. The duration of the treatment must be adjusted to the peculiarity of the seed, and the proper length of treatment can be discovered only by a careful course of experimentation. Inattention to this matter may result in utter failure.

3. But the chief cause of failure, the

cause of 90 per cent. of the bad failures, is in the drying. After electrification the seed must be dried ; and it must be dried to just the right extent and at just the right temperature. If the seed is insufficiently dried, it will be apt to heat if it is kept in bulk, or even in the sack, and then may begin to germinate before it is sown ; or, if it heats sufficiently, its germinating power may be destroyed. Even if it does not heat, it may be mildewed. If it is not kept, but is sown at once, it may be too much swollen with moisture to pass through the drill. If, on the other hand, it is over-dried, the seed is weakened in its germinating energy, or may even be killed. Again, if it is dried at too high a temperature, it may be baked or even scorched, and in either case it is killed. The drying is a very important part of the process, and, when the process fails to give an increase in the crop, the fault is usually in the drying.

Another source of failure is in delaying the sowing of the seed. The effect of the electro-chemical process on the seed is transient. After a time it passes away, so that, if the seed is kept too long out of the ground, it reverts to its previous condition, and no effect from the electrification can be expected. If the seed is kept in a dry place, the effect lasts about a month ; but toward the end of a month the effect passes off, and seed sown after this time must not be expected to show much improvement in the crop. It has happened during the war, when electrifying stations were few, that seed had to be sent a considerable distance for treatment, and a month was consumed by the return journey. In this case the increase in the yield, which, if the seed had been sown promptly, might have been expected to be 25 or 30 per cent., was only 5 per cent. Here again the process itself could not be justly blamed.

CHAPTER V

DISADVANTAGES

BESIDES occasional failures, the causes of which can almost always be traced, and found to be either in the faulty performance of the process, or in delay in the sowing, or in inequality of the conditions under which the treated seed and the control seed is sown and cultivated, there are certain disadvantages at present in the process, some of which are inherent, while others will be removed as it becomes better understood. Fortunately, none of them is sufficiently important to detract seriously from the benefits that the process confers. They are as follows :—

In the first place, another operation is added to those necessary for the cultivation of the farm. On the other hand, the burden of this process does not fall upon the farmer. He does not need to learn how to conduct it. It is done for him. It requires from him no extra skill, no extra labour, no new operation, no additional machine or implement, no more house-room, no addition to his expenses beyond the fee for treating his seed, which is in most cases trifling in comparison with the advantage he gains.

Secondly, it involves the delay of a day or two in sowing, and this may have some importance in view of the vicissitudes of the weather. If the farmer does not send his seed for treatment until the sowing season is actually upon him, he may miss the best days for sowing, and be compelled to sow when the land is not in as good condition as in might have been. The remedy is manifest. He should send his seed in good time. Electrifying stations are now sufficiently numerous to ensure that the farmer will not have to send his seed to any great distance, and sufficiently well equipped to ensure that his seed will be treated and returned promptly.[1] In time, travelling plants will be installed, which will go round from farm to farm and treat the seed upon the spot, in the farmer's own stackyard ; and by this means time will be saved and trouble abolished.   In any case, the farmer has a margin of time of about a month before he need sow his treated seed ; and although the sooner it is sown after treatment the better, yet if he has his seed treated early in the season, so as to have it ready before the time for sowing actually arrives, he will not miss a favourable opportunity.

Thirdly, the results are not uniform ; but it is necessary to explain what this means.   The results are uniform in this

---

[1] Experience since this was written shows that it is stated too absolutely. The rush of orders for the spring sowing of 1919 has been so great that the plant installed has proved insufficient, and orders for the electrification of hundreds of sacks have had to be refused. Electrifying plants are rapidly being enlarged and multiplied.

respect, that all the seed electrified at one operation and sown in similar soil will give uniform results ; but if part of the seed is sown in one kind of soil and part in another, the two crops are likely to differ. One will show more advantage than the other. Again, the increase in the crop on one farm is most in the grain, and in another is most in the straw. The increase in one crop may be eighteen or twenty bushels to the acre, and in another may be only five or six. In these respects the results are not uniform, and the reasons for these discrepancies are yet to be discovered, and no doubt will be discovered when there has been time for the necessary investigations ; and then the want of uniformity can be remedied. But the result is uniform in this respect : that there always is an increase in the crop that grows from the electrified seed. The increase may be in the number of grains in the ear, or in the number of culms grown from each seed, or in the length and stoutness and weight of the straw ; but in one or other or all of these respects the crop is increased. In that respect the results are uniform.

In the fourth place, as already explained, the effect upon the seed is not permanent. In the course of time it passes away, so that the seed will not show any benefit if it is kept too long after it has been treated and before it is sown. It is no use having seed treated in the autumn for sowing in the following spring. It must be sown within a month from the time of treatment. But a month is a sufficient margin, and few farmers will want more in ordinary seasons.

Lastly, if the process is not properly carried out, it will very probably fail to show any increase in the resulting crop; and if the treatment is very faulty, the grain may be damaged, and the crop will then suffer in consequence. This cannot justly be considered a disadvantage of the process itself. The process is a simple one, and is no more difficult to carry out success-fully than the process of dyeing a parcel of yarn, or sterilising a surgical dressing, and is much simpler than making a Stilton cheese ; but, like all these processes, it is not foolproof. It may be bungled, and it is very likely to be bungled if it is conducted by inexperienced or careless hands. It is simple, but it requires vigilant attention, proper conditions, and a certain skill that is to be attained only by practice under a skilled instructor. If these conditions are not observed, the grain may be damaged, and the process may fall into undeserved discredit. In fact, it has fallen into undeserved discredit in certain quarters, in consequence of faulty performance due to want of experience and want of skill in the performers ; but it cannot be too strongly insisted upon that in every case in which the result has been unsatisfactory the failure has been traced either to á fault in the method of performing the process, or to undue delay in sowing the seed, or to difference in the conditions under which the treated and the control crops were grown. To this rule there has been no exception whatever. Mistakes have been made. In an entirely new process it is inevitable that mistakes should be made ; and in certain quarters the reputation of the process has suffered because early and experimental trials, all of which could not be expected to be successful, were taken for examples of a matured and perfected process that ought never to fail. The process is now matured with respect to cereals, and with them it does not fail ; but before it was matured there were failures which were then unaccountable, but have since been explained.

CHAPTER VI

HORTICULTURAL SEEDS

THE inventor of the Wolfryn electro-chemical process took for the subject of his early experiments the chief seeds used in agriculture. The choice was natural, and was wise. Agricultural crops are by far the most important crops, and the most abundant crops; and of agricultural crops, the three standard cereals, wheat, oats, and barley, are by far the most important. As the experiments proceeded, the world was threatened with a scarcity of food; and if these crops could be materially increased, much would be done to relieve this scarcity. Moreover, the three cereals are much alike; they all belong to the same natural order of plants, they are easily procured in abundance, and they are grown upon a large scale almost everywhere in these islands. For all these reasons, cereals were chosen for the first subjects of experiment.

The last consideration, the scale on which they are grown, is especially important. An acre is a small area in the eyes of an agriculturist, and a single experiment, in which the yield of one acre is compared with the yield of another, is to the practical farmer of only trifling magnitude, and carries but little weight ; but in an acre of wheat there are between a million and a half and two millions of wheat plants ; and what an experiment conducted upon an acre of ground gives, when compared with the yield of another acre, is the average yield of at least a million and a half of plants compared with the average yield of another million and a half. Experiments upon this scale cannot be conducted in the laboratory ; experiments on this scale are rare in the practice of experimentation ; and experiments in which the average of such enormous numbers is taken must carry weight. Such numbers completely eliminate the disturbing effects of individual peculiarities in the seeds.

For all these good and sufficient reasons, agricultural seeds, and especially the seeds of cereals, received first attention, and horticultural seeds were relegated to the second place, and left over for subsequent experimentation ; but now that the proper treatment of cereals has been sufficiently ascertained to assure an increase in the crop in every case in which the process is properly conducted and the comparison fairly made, the inventor is turning his attention to horticultural seeds.

The field of experimentation opening out in this direction is enormous and inexhaustible. Horticultural seeds are twenty times, perhaps fifty times, as numerous as agricultural seeds, and are also very much more diverse. They belong to a much greater number of natural orders, and to orders that are much more widely different, and must engage the attention of many experimenters for many years. A beginning has been made, however, and some excellent results have been obtained ; but it must be clearly understood that the electro-chemical treatment of horticultural seeds is still in the experimental stage, and will not be recommended for general adoption for any one kind of seed until practical certainty of success with that kind of seed has been attained.

Meantime, the claims of agricultural seeds are still urgent and still clamant. From all parts of the world—from places as far distant as New Mexico, North Borneo, Nyasaland, South Africa, Trinidad, New Zealand, India, Japan, and elsewhere—the inventor receives urgent requests to explain the proper treatment for rice, sorghum, flax, sugar-cane, cotton, tobacco, and many other crops; and while horticultural seeds must be attended to, the claims of agricultural crops must take precedence. Manifestly, to settle the proper treatment of all these seeds, and at the same time to carry out the business organisation of the process in this and other countries, and to attend to the ever-increasing mass of inquiries and correspondence on the subject, is beyond the power of any one man, especially of a man approaching his eightieth year. This being so, and since the existing agricultural colleges display no inclination to take the matter in hand, their time being fully occupied, no doubt, with other affairs, it is Mr Fry's intention to establish, as soon as circumstances permit, a thoroughly equipped laboratory, on a sufficient area of ground, with a staff of skilled and trained experimenters to carry out investigations under his own eye, and determine the optimum treatment for every kind of seed.

No doubt, when this can be done, principles will be established and rules laid down that will materially shorten the time that need be spent over any one kind of seed. Indeed, from the experiments already made, which are very numerous, principles are beginning to emerge, and it is possible to begin the treatment of a new seed with some approximate guess as to the proper time, the proper strength of solution, and so forth ; and further experience will narrow the limits within which the treatment may be begun. But the problem with respect to horticultural seeds is in its infancy, and, while the inventor will welcome the co-operation of gardeners in growing treated seeds alongside of untreated seeds in the most various conditions, it must be distinctly understood that such trials are at present purely experimental ; that failures are to be looked for and expected ; and that the process is not to be condemned and abandoned because, with horticultural seeds, failures occasionally occur. If every experiment were successful at first trial, there would be little need of experiment. The only safe road to discovery is the road of trial and error ; and it is out of repeated errors that success at last emerges.

The conditions under which living things grow and thrive are so immensely complex that a result cannot be guaranteed with perfect confidence in every case ; but every farmer, every gardener, and every man of common-sense will admit that if a certain treatment, compared with controls, is followed in 80 per cent. of a large number of trials by a certain result which does not occur in the controls, that result is due to that treatment. In the case of cereals, substantial increase in the crop has followed the electro-chemical treatment in much more than 80 per cent. of the cases in which it has been fairly tried ; and when it is successful in 80 per cent. of trials of any horticultural seed, then, and not till then, it will be recommended for general adoption for that kind of seed. Premature publication of individual and sporadic successes as evidence of general success is much to be deprecated. It leads to anticipations that may not be fulfilled in other cases, and thus may throw undeserved discredit on a valuable process. When the inventor recommends the adoption of the process for any particular kind of seed, it may be relied upon to produce an increase of the crop in at least 80 per cent. of cases in which that seed is sown ; but even in these cases no specific amount or proportion of increase can be guaranteed. All that our present experiençe warrants us in predicting is that the proportion of increase is likely to range, on the average, about 30 per cent.

CHAPTER VII

THE EXPLANATION

OF the remarkable effect that electrification of seed has in increasing the vigour and yield of the crop that grows from the seed thus treated there can be no doubt, but by what means this effect is brought about is at present a matter of speculation. Several hypotheses present themselves, and some at least of these are susceptible of verification by observation and experiment ; and, as the matter is attracting much attention among students of bio-chemistry and in botanical laboratories, it is probable that before long a good deal of light will be thrown upon it.

The facts are :—

1. That by electrification the seed is altered in some way that causes it to grow

more vigorously, and to yield a larger growth.

2. That the effect on cereals is sometimes to produce a greater yield of grain, sometimes to produce a greater yield of straw, sometimes to have both of these effects; very rarely to increase the straw apparently at some expense to the yield of grain; less rarely to increase the yield of grain at some expense to the growth of straw; and frequently to increase the yield of both grain and straw, but in different proportions in different cases, although the treatment was, as far as could be judged, the same in all these cases.

3. That the effect is transitory, so that if the sowing of the seed is delayed for more than a month after the electrification, the effect is diminished, and, if the sowing is much delayed, may be wholly lost.

4. Some seeds, such as cereals, respond readily to the treatment, and rarely fail to show an increased yield in the subsequent crop. Other seeds, such as Leguminosæ,

appear to be refractory to the treatment, and up to the present time have shown sometimes little and sometimes no increase in the resulting crop.

5. Even seed of the same kind, oats or barley for instance, shows .very different results in different cases, although the treatment is, as far as can be judged, the same. One crop yields a very large increase after electrification, another parcel of similar seed yields a very small increase.

These are the facts to be explained. What is the explanation ? What hypotheses suggest themselves as capable of explaining all the facts ? For, however satisfactorily an hypothesis may explain some of them, it must be rejected unless it accounts for them all.

The obvious explanation, which the experienced experimenter will be inclined to regard with suspicion just because it is obvious, is that the electrification adds to the store of energy contained in the seed, which, since it contains more energy, acts more energetically. For a seed, like every other living thing, contains. not only a certain quantity of matter, but also a certain quantity of energy animating the matter. This is the difference between a live thing and a dead thing. If a live seed is heated to a certain temperature, it will be killed. It will be to all outward seeming the same as before. It will look the same and weigh the same. It will contain the same quantity of matter, and the matter will consist of very much the same quantities of the same elements in very much the same combinations ; but if we sow this seed under even the most favourable conditions, it will not germinate. Instead of germinating, it will decay. That is to say, instead of assimilating new matter and new energy, and building up its material structure into new and more elaborate combinations, it will fall to pieces, and subside into less and less elaborate and complicated structures, which lose their cohesion, separate from one another, and exist merely as chemical combinations and no longer as an organised structure. These chemical substances contain energy, it is true, but only enough energy to hold them together in those combinations. They do not contain the additional charge of available energy that is capable of building them up into more elaborate and complicated structures. They are dead, and this is the difference between life and death, between living things and dead things. Dead things contain only enough energy to keep them as they are: living things contain in addition enough energy to add to the complication of their structure, and to enable them to absorb and assimilate from without both matter and energy for this purpose.

Now, electricity is, from one aspect, a mode of energy. If it is a mode of motion, it is energy. If it is particulate, its particles are in motion, and so contain or convey energy ; and in either case, if we pass electricity into a substance, we add to the energy in that substance, and this energy is as it were detached, free, and additional to that previously contained in the substance. It is, therefore, a plausible and inviting hypothesis to suppose that the energy thus imparted to the seed may reinforce and reinvigorate what we may term, without committing ourselves to any theory, the vital energy of the seed, and so enable it to grow more vigorously and bring forth fruit more abundantly. The hypothesis is simple and attractive, but will it cover all the facts? Scarcely. It is difficult on this hypothesis to account for the discrepancies of the results in different cases. It is difficult to account for the increased yield being sometimes in the grain and sometimes in the straw. It is difficult to account for the small effect the process has upon Leguminosæ. It is difficult to account for the endurance of the effect for a month or more, and for its disappearance after this time is elapsed. Each of these effects may no doubt be explained by straining the hypothesis in this direction and in that, and by adding subsidiary hypotheses; but the necessity of doing so at once throws doubt upon the main hypothesis. It resembles on a small scale the prodigious framework of what is called Mendelism, in which hypothesis is piled on hypothesis, supposition on supposition, and assumption on assumption, until the mind reels under the accumulation. Pelion is piled upon Ossa, and the two are supported upon a slender stalk too fragile to bear the weight, and the whole structure collapses by reason of its top-heaviness. We must look round for something more plausible.

It is now well known that the whole superficial crust of the earth swarms with bacteria, and that some of these bacteria have very great influence, for evil or for good, upon the lives of higher organisms. The bacilli of tuberculosis and anthrax, and the vibrio of cholera, are cases in point. Plants also have their parasitic bacteria, some of which are destructive or deleterious to the plant on which they are parasitic, and others, such as the well-known azotobacter and *B. radicicola*, are beneficial. Electricity may have, and in fact is known to have, an influence on the growth of bacteria, and it is possible that it may stimulate and assist the growth of the nitrifying bacteria, and perhaps kill or inhibit the growth of those that are inimical to the growth of the plant. This is a plausible speculation, but it is only a speculation, and has little support from what is known ; neither does it fit in with all the facts that are to be explained. Neither azotobacter nor *B. radicicola* is known to occur in seeds, nor is either of them parasitic upon cereals ; nor is it known that either of them is stimulated into greater activity by electricity. We are here in the region of pure speculation, unsupported by any groundwork of fact, and it is not worth while to pursue researches in this direction until all else fails.

Again, it is well known that plants of all kinds are subject to the attacks of fungi, some of which are very deadly in their effects. Cereals, especially, suffer much from fungous diseases. It is necessary to mention only the smut, bunt, and rust of wheat, ergot of rye, and mildew, which attacks all cereals and many other plants as well. Smut, bunt, and mildew undoubtedly infest the surface of the seed grain, and may perhaps penetrate the interior ; and consequently it is a recognised and prevalent custom to spray seed corn with a solution of sulphate of copper in order to kill the adherent spores. It is evident that the steeping of the grain in a solution of some metallic salt, which is part of the Wolfryn process, will tend to destroy the spores on the surface of the grain, and that the ions, which are driven into the seed by the electric current, may destroy any spores that may have penetrated into the interior of the seed, and thus protect the plant against funguous attacks ; but this is not what we are in search of. There is no evidence that the superior yield of the plants grown from electrified seed is due to this freedom from fungous attacks to which the unelectrified plants are subject. The advantage is still gained when both crops are free from any disease. It is true that there is a certain amount of evidence, not yet enough to enunciate formally, that the electrifying process does diminish the liability of plants to be attacked by fungous diseases ; but this would not account for the increase of the crop over that of a crop that is free from disease. We must seek some other explanation.

The hypothesis that I suggest provisionally is rather more complicated than any of the foregoing, but it has the merit that it is not inconsistent with any of the known facts, and does account for them all in a fairly satisfactory manner without very much aid from subsidiary and auxiliary hypotheses. It will need a little more space for its statement, and it must be admitted at once that it is sadly in need of substantiation ; but it is quite susceptible of being substantiated or disproved by appropriate research, and this is no small merit in an hypothesis.

Although the power of vitamine was discovered in 1772 by Captain Cook, it is fewer than twenty years since the name was attached to the substance, and fewer years still since a vitamine was isolated and made visible separately from other things ; but by this time everybody knows what vitamines are, and has some notion of their properties. They belong to a much larger class of substances, some of which occur in various articles of food, and others are elaborated in the animal body itself, but all have certain properties in common. All of them are necessary for the healthy balance of nutrition of the body. If any one is absent, the nutrition of the body fails or goes wrong in a certain definite way, depending on the particular substance that is absent from the blood. If one is absent, the gums swell, become spongy, and bleed, the nutrition of the body fails in certain ways, and the person dies. If another is absent, the body becomes dropsical, the nerves fail to perform their functions, the heart fails, and the person dies. If yet another is absent, the skin atrophies, the hair falls out, the mind decays, the person becomes demented, and at length dies. If another substance is absent, the proper characters of sex are not assumed, and the person remains for life in the neutral sexual condition of childhood. If a male, he grows no beard, and his voice retains its thin, piping, childish pitch ; if a female, the hips remain narrow and the breasts never develop. Among these substances are some which regulate growth in infancy and childhood. If one of these substances is absent, the growth of different parts of the body is disproportionate. Certain parts of the body—the brain, for instance—remain undeveloped, and never progress beyond an early stage. If another is absent, the whole body is dwarfed, the person never grows up, but remains for life with the body of an infant. Some of these substances are, as I have said, elaborated in the body itself, usually in certain special organs, which have no other function ; others of them are provided by the food, that is, by certain articles of food ; but all have in common the property that their powers are exerted by almost incredibly small quantities. A man of 150 lbs. in weight is kept in robust health by two or three grains per diem of one of these substances. If these two or three grains are wanting, he sickens and dies : if they are provided, he is preserved in vigorous life. A pound contains 7000 grains, so that one or two millionth parts of his body-weight of one of these vitamines is enough to sustain a man in robust health : the continued absence of these one or two millionths of his weight is fatal.

Nor is it only animals that depend for their lives and their growth upon the incorporation into their bodies of extremely minute quantities of very complex substances. Plants also have their vitamines, which are called, not vitamines, but auximones; and, as in the case of animals, these accessory food-substances have a profound influence upon the growth of the plant. We may provide an animal with what appears to be a physiologically perfect diet, containing in ample quantity and in due proportion all the protein, carbohydrate, fat, and salts that are necessary to its life and growth ; but if we do not provide the necessary vitamines, the animal will neither grow nor live. And similarly, we may provide a plant in ample quantity and due proportion with all the necessary potash, phosphates, nitrogen, and salts that are required for its growth and nourishment ; but if it has not its necessary quantity of auximones, it will not thrive, and presumably, if we could deprive it of its auximones, it would not live.

The extraordinary results that have been attained by Professor Bottomley by the use of bacterised peat appear to be owing, without doubt, to the additional supply of auximones that his bacterised peat supplies to the plants ; and by whatever means we could increase the supply of auximones, by those means we could increase the vigour of the plant and the abundance of its products. The seed of every plant contains a store of nourishment for the supply of the seedling until it can gather its nourishment from the soil or the air in which it grows. Some seeds are of microscopic dimensions, and contain but little nourishment ; others, such as the broad bean, and still more the cocoanut, are of considerable size, and contain much ; but all contain some. And as the milk of mammals is a perfect physiological food, containing all the ingredients, including the vitamines, necessary for the nourishment, growth, and development of the infant mammal, so the albumen of the seed contains all the nourishment, including the auximones, necessary for the nourishment, growth, and development of the seedling plant.

We have seen that the function of one of the animal vitamines—it is not called a vitamine, for it is produced within the animal body, and therefore receives another name—is to enable the animal to attain the dimension proper to its species and race. If this particular vitamine is deficient, the animal, like Peter Pan, never grows up, but remains throughout its life of infantile stature and development. If this particular vitamine is in excess, the animal grows too much, and develops into a giant. Plants as well as animals have their vitamines, and one of these vitamines regulates the stature of the plant. If it is deficient, the plant never grows up. It remains, if not infantile, yet dwarfed ; and dwarfing is one of the most frequent varieties of very many species and races of plants. On the other hand, if we could supply the plant with an extra quantity of this particular vitamine or auximone, there is no reason to doubt that we could produce in it an earlier and more luxurious development.

We may pursue this line of speculation a little farther. It is established beyond doubt that there is one substance that conduces to the attainment by animals of mere size, and another that regulates the time and degree of development, especially of sexual development, so that, when this latter vitamine is wanting, sexual differentiation never takes place, and the animal remains permanently in the neutral state of childhood. On the other hand, cases sometimes occur in which this vitamine is produced in excess or prematurely, and then the animal undergoes premature sexual development, so that the boy of seven or eight grows a beard and his voice deepens into an unnatural bass, and the girl at even an earlier age attains puberty and becomes a premature woman. That wide variations occur in animals in fruitfulness and other sexual properties, and that these variations have little correlation with variations in size and in development in other respects, is well known.

Now, I think it is fair to suppose that an analogous state of things obtains in plants also. Like animals, plants increase at first solely in size and in structural complexity. Like animals, plants, when a certain size and structural complexity are attained, become sexually complete and reproduce their kind. Like animals, plants occasionally remain dwarfed in stature, occasionally attain premature sexual completion, and vary much in fertility and in other sexual characters, such as the size, colouring, doubleness, and so forth of their flowers. It is therefore fair to suppose that, as in animals, so in plants, development in size and vigour may be regulated by one vitamine, and development in sexual characters by another. If we grant this, we have an explanation of the undoubted fact that one apple tree runs chiefly to wood, while another produces fruit several years earlier, and much more abundantly. We then see why one crop of corn runs chiefly to straw, while another with less luxuriant growth produces more grain.

These vitamines, auximones, or whatever we please to call them, are extremely complex bodies ; but that they have a more or less definite chemical constitution is shown by the fact that they can be isolated by chemical processes and obtained in crystalline form. They are also closely allied in chemical constitution ; and the experience of chemists is that, in building up in the laboratory complex bodies of very similar chemical constitution, differing only by an atom of this or an atom of that, or having the same number of atoms differently arranged, the processes by which these different bodies are formed are closely similar, and sometimes result in a mixture of two or more similar bodies.   Moreover, it is a commonplace of laboratory knowledge that electricity has a powerful effect in disturbing and altering chemical combinations.

Taking all these facts together, I build upon them the following hypothesis.   The action of electricity upon a seed is to modify the chemical constitution of certain constituents of what is called the albumen of the seed.   Among these constituents are the auximones necessary to the growth and development of the plant, and these auximones differ but slightly from one another and from other constituents of the albumen, so that under certain conditions the auximones are constituted out of the albumen.

The effect of the electricity is, as I take it, so to act upon the albumen as to produce more of the auximones. These, though they differ profoundly in their effect upon the plant, are closely alike in their chemical constitution, so that some very trifling difference in the intensity or duration of the electric current, or perhaps in the strength of the saline solution in which the seed is steeped, may determine whether the increase is in the auximone that determines growth or in that which determines fertility. If the first is increased, the result will be a stronger and taller plant, with greater tillering and more sturdy straw. If the other auximone is increased, the result will be greater fertility, and a more copious production of seed.

Now let us apply this hypothesis to the facts and see if they are consistent with it. We have already seen that it is consistent with the facts that the growth of the plant is more vigorous and that it produces more grain when the seed has been electrified, and it is consistent with the fact that the increase is sometimes in the tillering and in the length and sturdiness of the straw, and sometimes in the yield of grain ; sometimes in both, and sometimes in one at the expense of the other. All these facts fit in very well with the hypothesis.

The next fact to be accounted for is that the effect of electrification upon the seed is transitory. This is quite consistent with the other hypotheses, and is consistent with this also ; for these auximones are bodies of extremely complicated chemical constitution —so complicated that their true nature and chemical structure have not yet been determined. The more complicated the chemical structure of a substance, the more unstable it is, other things being equal, and the more readily its constitution is altered ; the more readily it parts with an atom here and a molecule there, and changes into something else. Now, one of the conditions most favourable to the decomposition of all organic bodies is the presence of moisture, and it is therefore significant that, if we wish to preserve the change, whatever it is, that is produced in the seed by electricity, we must keep the seed dry. Damp seed reverts to its pre-electrified condition more rapidly than dry seed. The fact that the effect is transient fits the hypothesis, therefore, very well.

The fourth fact to be accounted for is that some seeds, such as those of cereals, respond readily to the electrical treatment, and show increases, sometimes very great increases, in the crops they produce, while upon other seeds, such as Leguminosæ, little or no effect has yet been produced. In explanation of this, it is certain that the chemical constitution of the " albumen " of cereals is widely different from that of the " albumen " of leguminous seeds. The latter, for instance, contain much more protein, and the protein they contain is very different from the gluten of wheat or the protein of barley or oats. But there is another and more significant difference. Of all plants that have been tested, Ieguminous plants contain the largest proportion of auximone. This auximone is distributed throughout the plant, and is elaborated by the plant in the course of its growth. The same thing occurs in other plants, but, as it would appear, they do not need so much as the highly organised Ieguminous plants, and therefore do not produce as much. From this it seems to follow that a small addition to the native auximone—and the amount produced in the seed can be but small—would produce less effect upon a Ieguminous plant, which already contains much, than upon a plant of a different kind that contains but little. Here again the hypothesis seems to be consistent with the fact of observation.

Lastly, the effect of the electric treatment, even when carried out in the same way upon the same kind of seed, varies within very wide limits, increasing sometimes the straw, sometimes the grain, and the increase being sometimes as little as 4 or 5 per cent., and sometimes as much as 60 or 70 per cent.   As to this, there are two things to be said.   In the first place, it has been found in experience that different seeds, even of closely allied family, require very different lengths of treatment to produce the best effects.   Barley, for instance, requires twice as long as oats.   To people who have no experience of agriculture, wheat is wheat, barley is barley, and oats are oats ; but agriculturists and seed merchants know that there are quite 150 different kinds of wheat in cultivation, all differing from one another in some more or less important respect ; and if wheat and barley take, as they do, such very different lengths of treatment to pro- duce the best effect, it is highly probable that different kinds of wheat require different lengths of treatment—lengths that do not differ as widely as that of barley does from that of wheat, but still lengths that are material.

Again, it is known to millers that dif- ferent varieties of wheat have very different physical constitutions, behave very differently in the mill, and yield their products in different proportions and of different qualities. These physical peculiarities are accompanied, and to some extent conditioned, by chemical peculiarities, and therefore it is not to be expected that the same electrical treatment will produce the same effect upon them all, especially when we consider how slight the differences between many of the different chemical constituents of the seed are. On these grounds, we should expect that the effects of the electrical treatment of seed would be diverse, and especially so if the effect is of the nature of a chemical change. There is nothing inconsistent with the hypothesis, therefore, in the diversity of effect that electricity produces on different samples of seed that are called by the same name. It is quite likely, moreover, that the effect may vary according to the physical condition of the seed at the time of treatment, and according to the physical conditions under which it has been kept. The chemical changes that take place in seeds are subtle and elusive, and very little is known of them ; but it may be presumed with some confidence that one sample of seed will differ in chemical constitution, and therefore in its chemical reactions, from another sample grown in the same field at the same time, if, in the meantime, they have been stored under different conditions of dryness, temperature, and perhaps other respects.   Even the temperature of the bath in which the electrification takes place may very likely modify the effect of the electricity upon the chemical constitution of the complex substance that goes under the name of albumen.   There is nothing, therefore, in the diversified effect of the electricity upon the seed that is inconsistent with the hypothesis here advanced, and upon the whole it fits the facts fairly well, and better than any other that has yet been suggested.

Recently, a book that throws a flood of light on electro-physiology has been published by Mr Baines, an accomplished electrician. He has proved by many thousands of experiments, conducted with the most sensitive instruments that have yet been invented, that every plant, and every part of a plant, not only has electric capacity, but contains an electric charge. It is, in short, a charged electric cell ; and he has shown that this is as true of the seed as of every other distinct part of the plant. It seems that the proper performance of the function of each part of the plant is connected with the possession of this charge of electricity ; and it requires no great effort of reasoning to see that, if this is so, the greater the electric charge, the more vigorously will the function be performed. One of Mr Baines' experiments is a very remarkable confirmation of those of Mr Fry. Mr Baines cooked two potatoes. One he boiled for fifteen minutes, and the other he baked for the same length of time. After this treatment, one would naturally suppose that the potatoes were dead, and no gardener in his senses would expect them to show any sign of life.   Nor would they have shown any sign of life if Mr Baines had left them alone ; but instead of leaving them alone he passed into them for twenty-four hours a feeble current of electricity, and thereafter both the potatoes sprouted in a remarkable manner.   It was remarkable that they should sprout at all, and that they did so is striking evidence of the efficacy of Mr Fry's system. After this, objections to the electrification of seeds on the ground that *a priori* it is not likely to improve the vigour of germination are out of court.   It is true that a potato is not a seed, but it acts the part of a seed in farming operations ; and Mr Fry has found that the electrification of seeds and of " seed " potatoes may be carried on on the same lines and will produce similar effects.